The Story of a Special Day
Volume 209

July
27

The 208th day of the year (209th in leap years). There are 157 days remaining until the end of the year.

by Michael Dobson

Timespinner
Press

This book is (or will be) available in e-book form for Kindland other formats from your favorite online booksellers.

For more information about the series, about us, or about your special day, please email us at editor@timespinnerpress.com.

Look for other volumes in *The Story of a Special Day,* coming often. See www.timespinnerpress.com for details and for the most recent information.

Table of Contents

Cover: Macbeth, by Thomas Beach. The historical Macbeth was defeated by Malcolm Canmore on July 27, 1054 — the **EVENT OF THE DAY**.

Quote of the Day

"Macbeth shall never vanquish'd be, until Great Birnam wood to high Dunsinane hill Shall come against him."

Macbeth (Act IV, Scene 1, by William Shakespeare The historical Macbeth was defeated by Malcolm Canmore on July 27, 1054.

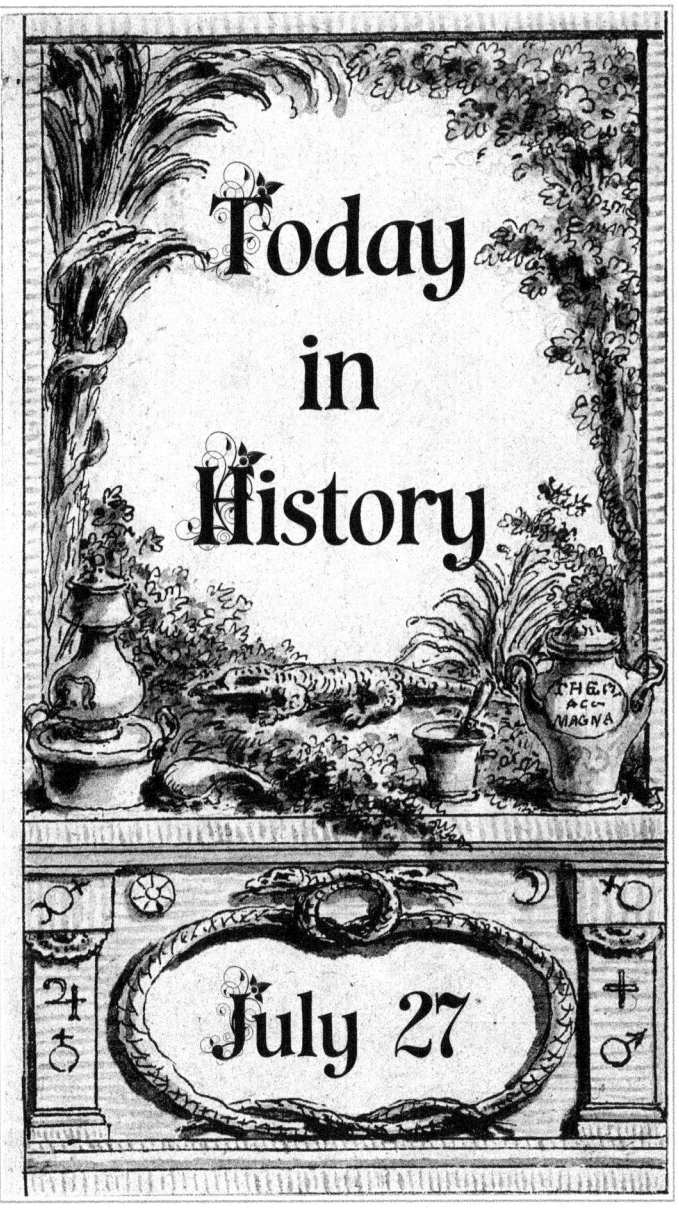

Today in History

July 27

Macbeth, from *Scotland's Story* by H. E. Marshall

Event of the Day
July 27, 1054—Macbeth Defeated at Dunsinane

On July 17, 1054*, Macbeth, King of Scotland, was defeated in battle by Siward, Earl of Northumbria, in a bloody battle somewhere north of the Firth of Forth in Scotland. Today, of course, Macbeth is best known as a character in Shakespeare's play of the same name, but there was a historical Macbeth, whose story differs in significant respects from the play.

Macbeth, by John Hall

The person we know as the historical Macbeth was actually named Mac Bethad mac Findlaích in medieval Gaelic, which roughly translates as Macbeth MacFinley. Some sources say he was a grandson of King Malcolm II (the Malcolm of Shakespeare's play later became King Malcolm III);

---

* In fairness, it's often uncertain exactly what day an event nearly one thousand years ago took place, but there aren't any competing dates. Several different authorities we checked cite July 27; the rest just leave it as 1054. It would certainly have been in the summertime, when most military campaigns took place for weather reasons.

Illustration of Macbeth and Banquo encountering the witches from *Holinshed's Chronicles*, first published in 1577.

others say he was a cousin of Throfinn the Mighty, Earl of Orkney and Caithness.

When Malcolm II died in 1034, his son Duncan I took the throne. In Shakespeare's play, Duncan is an old man and Macbeth kills him to take the throne.

The real Duncan, however, was only in his mid-30s when he took the throne. After he lost a major battle, he lost support, and in retaliation invaded Macbeth's domain, Moray, in 1054. In the resultant battle, Duncan was killed and Macbeth became king. There was no opposition.

Meanwhile, there was conflict in England between the Earl of Wessex and King Edward the Confessor. Fleeing the battlefield, many exiles ended up in Macbeth's court. This did not sit well with the King of England, who ordered an attack. In a battle which reportedly killed 3,000 Scots and 1,500 English, Macbeth was defeated and fled, dying in battle two years later. His stepson Lulach was king for seven month before he was assassinated by Malcolm, who took the throne. King Malcolm III would rule for 35 years.

For his history plays, William Shakespeare often consulted *Holinshed's Chronicles*, a very detailed history of Britain but not considered very accurate by historians. Shakespeare took his own liberties with the story, and the Macbeth of the play is a very different person than the Macbeth of history. This was not unusual for Shakespeare, who sometimes liked to comment indirectly on current events.

Written during the reign of King James VI and I[†], who was also the royal patron of Shakespeare's own acting company, the plan in part reflects Shakespeare's relationship with the king. (James VI and I was supposedly a descendent of Banquo, who received the prophecy "Thou shalt get kings.)

There are echoes of the execution of Henry Garnet, a Jesuit priest who learned about the Gunpowder Plot while listening to a confession. Bound by the seal of the confessional, he did not notify the authorities (though he gave some hints to the church authorities). He was hanged, drawn, and quartered.

[†] Following the death of Queen Elizabeth I, the heir to the throne of England was James VI, King of the Scots, and son of Mary Queen of Scots. There had never been a king of England named James, so when the thrones of England and Scotland merged in 1603, he became James VI of Scotland and James I of England. Because he was king of Scotland first, it's written "James VI and I" instead of the other way around.

Macbeth is Shakespeare's shortest tragedy, around half the size of *Hamlet*. Some suggest that it was printed from a heavily cut prompt book, and may have been significantly altered from the original text. Some sixty years later, an adaptation by Sir William Davenant reintroduced the play to mass audiences, and his version was the standard for a long time. David Merrick claimed to produce the play "as written by Shakespeare," but changed it even more.

William Shakespeare, by William Blake

The play became so popular that when fans of two rival performances of *Macbeth* on Broadway in 1849 began fighting. In the resultant Astor Place Riot, 31 rioters were killed and more than 100 injured.

Many great actors have been associated with the play, including Edmund Kean, Charlotte Cushman, and Sir Laurence Olivier. The first film version was a 1905 short subject, *Death Scene From Macbeth*. Orson Welles filmed the play in 1948. Japanese director Akira Kurosawa adapted it as *Kumunosu-jo*, known in English as *Throne of Blood*. Roman Polanski filmed it again in 1971. In 1975, it was adapted into a comedy-thriller *Scotland, PA*, set in a fast-food restaurant. There have been more than 30 radio versions as well.

A famous theatrical superstition about *Macbeth* states it is bad luck to mention the play by name while inside a theater. As a result, actors may refer to it as "the Scottish play," "Mr. and Mrs. M," or the abbreviated "MacB." The play is supposedly cursed because Shakespeare used real witch spells in the text, and the witches didn't like it.

The Battle of Dunsinane, by John Martin (Macbeth and a companion watch the approaching Northumbrian army (Courtesy National Galleries of Scotland)

US General Mark Clark signs the Korean armistice agreement on July 27, 1953 (Courtesy US Navy Museum)

North Korean leader Kim Il-Sung signs the agreement.

What Happened on July 27?

From the creation of great works of engineering and art, to devastating wars and natural disasters, thousands of years of history have left their mark on each and every day of the year. Here are some important events that occurred on July 27. (Illustrated items are boxed.)

1794‡ — As the French Revolution's Reign of Terror comes to an end, Maximilian **Robespierre is arrested** in what becomes known as the Thermidorian Reaction. He is executed along with many of his supporters the following day.

The Arrest of Robespierre, by Jean-Joseph-François Tassaert

‡ The French Revolutionaries came up with their own calendar, so July 27 was known as the 9th day of the month of Thermidor.

1890 — Painter **Vincent van Gogh shoots himself;** he dies two days later.

1929 — The **Geneva Convention** is signed, establishing standards for the treatment of prisoners of war.

1949 — The **first commercial jetliner,** the de Havilland Comet, makes its maiden flight on the birthday of company founder Geoffrey de Havilland.

1953 — **Korean War fighting ends** with the signing of an armistice. There was no actual peace treaty, meaning that the two Koreas are still technically at war. *(Photos pg. 12)*

1974 — In the **Watergate scandal,** the Judiciary Committee of the US House of Representatives votes to approve the first article of impeachment against President Richard Nixon, who resigns on August 9.

American prisoners of war captured during the Battle of the Bulge, December 1944 (Courtesy Defense Imagery)

Quote of the Day

"I have always noticed that in portraits of really great writers the mouth is always firmly closed."

Gertrude Stein, poet and playwright
died July 27, 1946

Births
and
Deaths

July 27

Bob Hope (left) with Bing Crosby in the film Road to Bali (1952).
Bob Hope died at the age of 100 on July 27, 2003.

Notable July 27 People

With the current world population at about seven billion people, on average about 19 million people also celebrate their birthdays on July 27 — and that isn't counting the millions and millions who came before! No matter when you were born, you share your birthday with many special people whose accomplishments (and occasionally embarrassments) have been noted as part of history.

In this section, you'll meet fascinating people who share your birthday. They're organized by what they're famous for, and then in reverse chronological order from most recent to earliest. Those who are shown in photographs or artwork have a box around them. We don't have photos of everyone, so please forgive us if your favorite person is missing.

Some of these people you've heard of, others may be new to you, but they all make up an important part of the reason that July 27 is a truly special day!

The Assassination of Marat by Charlotte Corday, by Paul-Jacques-Aimé Baudry (Courtesy Musée des Beaux-Arts de Nantes)

Who Was Born on July 27?

Games and Hobbies

Gary Gygax, game designer and publisher best known as the co-creator of the pioneering roleplaying game *Dungeons & Dragons. (1938)*

Government and Politics

Charlotte Corday, known as the "Angel of Assassination," executed by guillotine during the French Revolution for assassinating Jacobin leader Jean-Paul Marat in his bathtub. *(1793)*

Jeremiah Dixon, surveyor best known for his partnership with Charles Mason in settling a boundary dispute between colonial Pennsylvania and Maryland by determining what was later called the Mason-Dixon Line. Dixon is thus the namesake of "Dixie," a term for the American South. *(1733)*

Journalism and Writing

Jack Higgins, best-selling author of espionage and thriller novels whose breakthrough hit was the 1975 book *The Eagle Has Landed. (1929)*

Vincent Canby, influential film and theater critic for the New York *Times* for nearly 30 years. *(1924)*

Hilaire Belloc, Anglo-French author, essayist, and poet who was one of the most prolific and popular writers in early 20th century England. *(1870)*

Giosuè Carducci, considered the national poet of modern Italy; first Italian to receive the Nobel Prize in Literature. *(1835)*

Music

Maureen McGovern, singer and actress whose best known hit was "The Morning After," from the 1972 film *The Poseidon Adventure. (1949)*

Bobbie Gentry, singer-songwriter and country crossover performer best known for her 1967 hit "Ode to Billie Joe." *(1944)*

Nick Reynolds, musician best known as a founding member of The Kingston Trio. *(1933)*

Performing Arts

Maya Rudolph, member of the *Saturday Night Live* cast for seven years, appeared in such films as *50 First Dates, A Prairie Home Companion*, and *Bridesmaids. (1972)*

Julian McMahon, Australian actor known internationally for roles in *The Fantastic Four* (and sequels), *Premonition*, and *Red*; as well as TV series such as *Home and Away, Charmed*, and *Nip/Tuck*. *(1968)*

Norman Lear (born July 27, 1922) created the groundbreaking sitcom *All in the Family* as well as many other shows.

Rahul Bose, Indian actor called "the superstar of Indian arthouse cinema" and "the Sean Penn of Oriental cinema." *(1967)*

Carol Leifer, four-time Emmy winning comedian and writer; the character Elaine in the sitcom *Seinfeld* was based on her. *(1956)*

Yahoo Serious, Australian actor and director best known for his 1998 comedy *Young Einstein. (1953)*

Simon Jones, actor best known for playing Arthur Dent in the television and radio versions of *The Hitchhiker's Guide to the Galaxy. (1950)*

Maury Chaykin, actor best known for playing detective Nero Wolfe in a series of made-for-TV movies. *(1949§)*

Betty Thomas, best known for her Emmy-winning role on the TV series Hill Street Blues; later a feature film director whose works include *The Brady Bunch Movie, Private Parts, Dr. Dolittle,* and *I Spy. (1947)*

John Pleshette, actor best known for his role in *Knots Landing* and as the title character in the TV movie *The Trial of Lee Harvey Oswald*; cousin of actress Suzanne Pleshette. (1942)

Don Galloway, actor best known for his role on the long-running television series *Ironside. (1937)*

---

§ Maury Chaykin died on the same day of the year as the date on which he was born.

Norman Lear, television writer and producer who created such sitcoms as *All in the Family, Sanford and Son, One Day at a Time, The Jeffersons, Good Times,* and *Maude. (1922) (Photo page 23.)*

Keenan Wynn, American character actor whose many films include *Requiem for a Heavyweight, Annie Get Your Gun, Dr. Strangelove, Point Blank,* and *The Great Race. (1916)*

Science and Technology

Sheikh Muszaphar Shukor, surgeon who became the first Malaysian commercial astronaut with a tour on the International Space Station. *(1972)*

Geoffrey de Havilland, aircraft designer who founded the de Havilland Aircraft Company. *(1882)*

Hans Fischer, German chemist who received the 1930 Nobel Prize for Chemistry for his researches in haemin (a molecule contained in hemoglobin) and chlorophyll. *(1881)*

Sports and Games

Jordan Spieth, professional golfer who achieved world number one rank; named by *Time* magazine on its 2016 list of "100 Most Influential People." *(1993)*

Alex Rodriguez (Photo: Glenn Brunette, CC BY-SA 2.0)

Alex Rodriguez, shortstop and third baseman nicknamed "A-Rod," considered one of the greatest players of all time, but his career was marred by his involvement in a scandal involving performance-enhancing drugs. *(1975)*

Jorge Arce, boxer who achieved world titles in four different weight divisions, nicknamed "the Mexican Cowboy." *(1979)*

Neil Brooks, won a gold medal in the 4x100m medley relay at the 1980 Olympic Games; suspended from international play for drinking 46 cans of beer on the return flight to Australia after the 1986 Commonwealth Games. *(1962)*

Jo Durie, professional tennis player ranked as high as World No. 5. *(1960)*

Hugh Green, NFL and college linebacker; played for the University of Pittsburgh, the Tampa Bay Buccaneers, and the Miami Dolphins; three-time consensus All-American and member of the College Football Hall of Fame. *(1959)*

Christopher Dean, Olympic gold medalist in ice dancing with his partner Jayne Torvill. *(1958)*

Allan Border, Australian cricketer who set world records in the most Test matches (156) and total Test runs (11,174), including 27 centuries; inducted into the ICC Cricket Hall of Fame. *(1955)*

Peggy Fleming, Olympic gold medal figure skater and three-time world champion, ranked as one of the most popular athletes in America. *(1948)* *(Photo pg. 28)*

Dennis Ralston, professional tennis player, 1987 inductee into the International Tennis Hall of Fame. *(1942)*

Ted Whitten, recognized as one of the all-time greatest players of Australian rules football, member of the Australian Football Hall of Fame and voted captain of the AFL's Team of the Century. *(1933)*

Leo Durocher, baseball player, manager, and coach; nicknamed "Leo the Lip" for his outspokeness and clashes with umpires and other officials; member of the Baseball Hall of Fame. He is widely credited with the saying "Nice guys finish last," although that is an edit of his original, longer quotatation. *(1905)*

A set of stamps from Paraguay featuring skater **Peggy Fleming**

Leo Durocher (left), with TV horse *Mister Ed* and actor Alan Young

Mohammad Reza Pahlavi (1939)

Who Died on July 27?

Crime and Punishment

John Friedrich, engineer and businessman who became known as "Australia's greatest conman" for a fraud involving over AUS$293 million. *(1991)*

Government and Military

Mohammad Reza Pahlavi (محمدرضا پهلوی), Shah of Iran from 1941 to 1979, when he was overthrown during the Iranian Revolution. *(1980)*

Claire Lee Chennault, US Army Air Corps general who commanded the Flying Tigers fighter group in the China-Burma-India theater of World War II. *(1917) (Photo page 32.)*

Journalism and Literature

James Alan McPherson, first African-Amerian writer to win the Pultizer Prize for Fiction; one of the initial recipients of the MacArthur Fellowship. *(2016)*

Gertrude Stein, novelist and poet who was one of the leading figures in the American expatriate community in early 20th century Paris, best known for her book *The Autobiography of Alice B. Toklas.* Also known for two quotes, "Rose is a rose is a rose is a rose," and "there is no there there," said to be a reference to Oakland, California. *(1946) (Photo pg. 33)*

General Claire Chennault (in leather jacket, standing next to the
propeller) with pilots of the 23rd Fighter Group

Mikhail Lermontov (Михаи́л Ле́рмонтов), known
as the "poet of the Caucasus" and the most
important literary figure of the Russian Romantic
period. *(1841 [O.S. July 15]**)*

** Russia changed from the Julian to the Gregorian calendar later
than the rest of Europe, and so some dates are given in both
"O.S." (Old Style, Julian) and "N.S." (New Style, Gregorian). N.S
July 27 is the same day as O.S. July 15. For more on calendar types,
see "What Day of the Week is July 27?"

Gertrude Stein (Photo: Carl Van Vechten)

James Mason, in the 1959 film *North by Northwest*

Music

Leon Wilkeson, bass player for Lynryd Skynyrd. *(2001)*

Bobby Day, musician and songwriter who wrote such hits as "Over and Over," "Little Bitty Pretty One," and "Rockin' Robin." *(1984)*

Performing Arts

Geoffrey Hughes, actor best known as Eddie Yeats on the British soap opera *Coronation Street. (2012)*

Maury Chaykin, actor best known for playing detective Nero Wolfe in a series of made-for-TV movies. *(2010††)*

Bob Hope, legendary comedian and actor famous for his USO shows that entertained American troops, for his "Road" pictures co-starring Bing Crosby, and for his signature song, "Thanks for the Memory." He died at the age of 100. *(2003)* *(Photo page 18)*

James Mason, actor whose many films include *Lolita, North by Northwest, Heaven Can Wait,* and *The Boys from Brazil. (1984)*

William Wyler, only film director to win three Best Picture Academy Awards, for *Ben-Hur, The Best Years of Our Lives,* and *Mrs. Miniver. (1981)*

---

†† Maury Chaykin died on the same day of the year as the date on which he was born.

Science

Emil Theodor Kocher, Swiss physician who received the 1909 Nobel Prize in Physiology or Medicine for his research into the thyroid. *(1917)*

John Dalton, English scientist who did pioneering work in atomic theory and in the area of color blindness. *(1844)*

Sports

Jack Tatum, NFL safety known as "the Assassin" for his aggressive playing style, including a tackle that paralyzed the other player from the chest down; member of tthe College Football Hall of Fame. *(2010)*

Rick Ferrell, baseball player, coach, and executive; member of the National Baseball Hall of Fame.

Frank Zamboni, inventor and businessman who invented the modern ice resurfacer that bears his name. *(1988)*

Travis Jackson, shortstop for the New York Giants from 1922 through 1936, member of the National Baseball Hall of Fame.

Smoky Joe Wood, pitcher and outfielder for the Boston Red Sox and Cleveland Indians. *(1985)*

Joe Tinker, baseball player best remembered for his double play combination with Johnny Evers and Frank Chance, often cited as "Tinker-to-Evans-to-Chance." Member of the National Baseball Hall of Fame. *(1917)*

Quote of the Day

"No people can live in the past - not even in its own past. But if it no longer has a link with its history, it must of necessity perish."

Mohammad Rezā Shāh Pahlavi
Shah of Iran, died July 27, 1980

Holidays
Around
the World

July 27

A Korean War veteran places a wreath at the Korean War Veterans Memorial, Washington, DC, on the 60th anniversary of the Korean War armistice agreement. **National Korean War Veterans Armistice Day** is comemmorated each year on July 27.

Holidays Around the World

If you're looking for a reason to take your special day off, you should know that every single day is a holiday somewhere in the world! Here's some of what you can celebrate on July 27!

Commemorations of the End of the Korean War

- **National Korean War Veterans Armistice Day** (United States)

- **Day of Victory in the Great Fatherland Liberation War** (North Korea)

(South Korea does not have a specific public holiday for July 27, but they celebrate Constitution Day on July 17.)

Fixed Celebrations

- **Araw ng Iglesia ni Cristo** (Iglesia ni Cristo Day, Philippines, celebrating the founding of the church of the same name.)

- **José Celso Barbosa Day** (Puerto Rico, celebrating the life and achievements of an early political leader of the Commonwealth.)

- **Ngày thương binh liệt sĩ** (Day for Martyrs and Wounded Soldiers, Vietnam

Moveable and Multi-Day Events

Some events take place over a specific week or time period. Start and finish dates may vary from year to year. Some events occur on different days each year (such as "fourth Saturday" of a given month). These events sometimes take place on July 27.

Fourth Sunday in July
- Parents' Day (US)

Second to Last Sunday in July
- Construction Holiday (Quebec)

Fourth Thursday in July
- National Chili Dog Day

Thursday before the First Monday in August
- Emancipation Day (Bermuda)

Friday Following Bermuda Emancipation Day
- Somer's Day (Bermuda)

Last Friday in July
- National Schools Tree Day (Australia)
- System Administrator Appreciation Day

Last Saturday in July
- National Dance Day (US)

Last Sunday in July
- Father's Day (Dominican Republic)
- National Tree Day (Australia)
- Navy Day (Russia)
- Reek Sunday (Ireland, a religious pilgrimage in which people climb Ireland's holiest mountain, Croagh Patrick)

Religious Feast Days and Holidays

Every religion normally has feast days and holidays associated with it. While some religious days take place on a given calendar day, others occur on different days each year, usually because the date is determined by the phases of the Moon rather than the Earth's path around the Sun. Here are some religious feasts, festivals, and holidays that sometimes or always fall on July 27.

Observances

Month of the Most Precious Blood of Jesus (Catholicism)

Saint Days

Each day in the year is considered a feast day for one or more saints. They are somewhat different in western Christianity (Catholicism and many forms of Protantism) and in eastern (Orthodox) Christianity.

In **Western Christianity,** July 27 is the feast day of Saints Aurelius, Natalia, and Pantaleon, as well as the Seven Sleepers of Ephesus.

In **Eastern Orthodox Christianity,** it is also the commemoration of Equal-to-the-Apostles Clement of Ohrid, and Saints Sabbas, Angelar, Nahum, Horasdus, Anthusa, Iosaph of Moscow, and Manuel. (These saints are honored on July 14 by Old Calendrists.‡‡)

---

‡‡ "Old Calendrists" use the Julian, rather than the Gregorian, calendar. For an explanation of different calendar types, see "What Day of the Week is July 27?"

In *Coptic Orthodox Christianity*, which uses its own calendar, July 27 is the equivalent of the 20th day of the month of Epip. They commemorate the martyrdom of Saint Theodore of Shotep.

Celebrations About Food

In the United States, almost every day of the year is dedicated to a particular food. (Some other countries also have official food days, but only in America is there one every single day!) Sponsored by manufacturers, retailers, farmers, or simply fans, these days are often proclaimed by the President, Congress, state governors, or mayors. Given that there are more different foods than days of the year, some days honor more than one kind of food!

Some foods just get a day, while others get a whole month. Here's what to eat on July 27 and the rest of the month of July!

July 27 is **National Scotch Day.** Scotch whisky (never "whiskey") is controlled according to the Scotch Whisky Regulations, governing ingredients, manufacturing, and aging. Most scotch is blended from different varieties; single-malt scotches come from a single distillery. While the origin of scotch is unknown, it shows up in government documents as early as 1495.

Various sources list the following foods promoted during the month of July:

- National Baked Beans Month
- National Blueberry Month
- National Candy Month

- National Culinary Arts Month
- National Fruit and Veggies Month
- National Grilling Month
- National Honey Month
- National Hot Dog Month
- National Ice Cream Month
- National Pickle Month
- National Picnic Month
- National Rosé Wine Month
- National Watermelon Month

A Ford Model A ice cream van at the Henry Ford Museum (Photo: Alf van Beem) — for **National Ice Cream Month**

Honorary Months

Presidents, Congresses, and nations around the world issue proclamations recognizing particular months to honor certain causes. These events generally fall in April, though honorary months do come and go.

Holidays established by states and nonprofit organizations are listed if verified. If not otherwise specified, all months are US. There is some variation from year to year; some celebratory months get added and others get dropped. Two places to get up to date information are the current edition of Chase's Calendar of Events *or the website Brownielocks. Here are some honorary designations for July.*

Health

- Bereaved Parents Awareness Month
- Fragile X Awareness Month
- Group B Strep Awareness Month (US, UK)
- Herbal/Prescription Interaction Awareness Month
- Juvenile Arthritis Awareness Month
- National Wheelchair Beautification Month

Recreation

- Family Golf Month
- National Park and Recreation Month
- National Vacation Rental Month
- Women's Motorcycle Month

Society

- Cell Phone Courtesy Month
- Get Ready for Kindergarten Month
- National Black Family Month

Just for Fun

Anybody can make up a holiday, and many people do. While none of these are officially recognized and some may come and go, here are a few more holidays for July 27.

- National Sleepy Head Day (Finland)
- Take Your Houseplant for a Walk Day (US)
- Walk on Stilts Day (US)

Los Zancos (The Stilts), by Francisco Goya
for **Walk on Stilts Day**

Quote of the Day

"The English winter — ending in July,
To recommence in August."

— Lord Byron, *Don Juan*

About
the
Month
of

July

July, from the *Brevarium Grimani* by Simon Bening (c.1510)

July: The Seventh Month

"Hot July brings cooling showers,
Apricots and gillyflowers."
— *Sara Coleridge, "The Months"*

In the original Roman calendar, the month of July was named *Quintilis*, the fifth month, because the Romans originally counted the first of March as the beginning of the new year.

Quintilis was renamed July by the Roman senate in honor of Gaius Julius Caesar after his death in 44 BCE, because Caesar, among his other accomplishments, had undertaken a major calendar reform, known as the Julian calendar, which remained the standard European calendar until 1582 CE. (Not to be outdone, Emperor Augustus arranged for the next month, Sextilis, to be renamed in his honor.)

July is one of the seven months with 31 days. In a common (non-leap) year, it always starts on the same day of the week as April, and on the same day of the week as January in leap years. Strangely, in common years, no other month of the year ends on the same day of the week as July! (In leap years, the last day of July and January fall on the same day.)

July in Other Cultures

In Latin, the month of July was spelled *Iulius*, as the Romans did not have the letter "J."

In Albanian, the month is *korrik*. Arabs call the month يوليه *(yūlia)*.

It is юли *(juli)* in Bulgaria, *lipanj* in Croatia, and *červen* in Czech.

The Finns call the month *kesäkuu* and the Greeks call it Ιούλιος *(Ioúlios)*.

The Hebrew calendar has different months, but when they refer to the Gregorian month, it's יולי *(yûlî)*.

In Gaelic, July is *Meitheamh mi an Mheitheamh*, and in Russian, it is июнь *(ijun')*.

The Chinese use 六月 *(liùyuè* in Mandarin); Koreans 유월 *(yuweol);* and it's 腩趏 *(tháng sáu)* in Vietnamese.

July Sayings and Superstitions

Farming

- The corn harvest will be good if the corn growing in the fields is "knee high by the Fourth of July."
- "If the first of July be rainy weather, 'twill rain more or less for four weeks together."
- "Rain or dry, plant your turnips on the Fourth of July."

- A swarm of bees in May is worth a load of hay. A swarm of bees in June is worth a silver spoon. A swarm of bees in July is not worth a fly.

Marriage

- "Those who in July do wed, must labor for their daily bread."

As for which day of the week, that's easy.

Monday for health, Tuesday for wealth, Wednesday best of all, Thursday for losses, Friday for crosses, Saturday for no luck at all.

July Symbols

Birthstone: Ruby (symbolizes success, devotion, and integrity.)

According to an old English proverb, "The glowing Ruby should adorn/Those who in warm July are born,/Then will they be exempt and free/From love's doubt and anxiety."

Ruby

Birth Flowers: Water Lily (purity of heart) or Larkspur (lightness and levity.)

Water Lily (Photo: Dinkum)

Birth Tree: Elm (strength of will and intuition)

"Study of an Elm Tree," John Constable (1821)

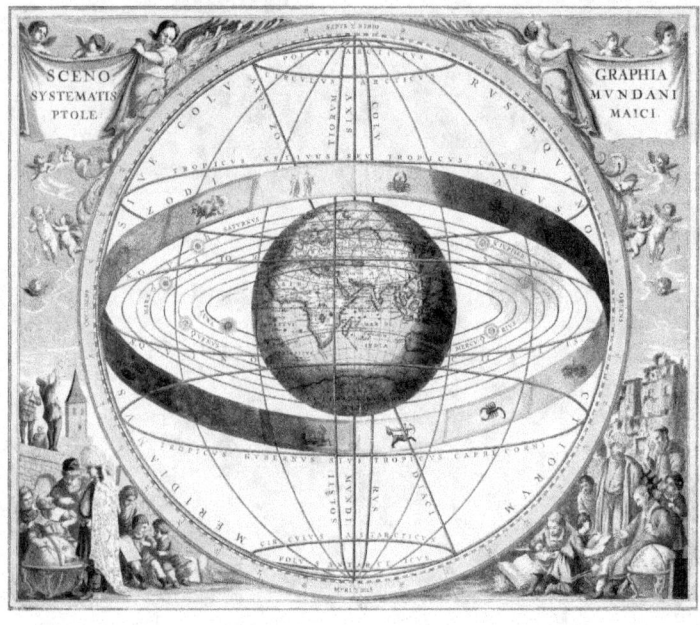

Scenography of the Ptolemaic Cosmography, by Johannes van Loon, based on Andreas Cellarius's *Harmonia Macrocosmica,* 1660

July 27 Zodiac Signs

From the perspective of someone on Earth, the Sun appears to move through the sky throughout the year, along a path astronomers call the *ecliptic plane*. The ecliptic plane is divided into twelve constellations, known as the zodiac, based on traditionally observed patterns of stars. On your birthday, you can't see your constellation, because it's in the daytime sky.

The zodiac was first developed by Babylonian astronomers about 2,500 years ago. Because they were unaware that the Earth wobbles like a spinning top (known as *precession*), they didn't make allowance for the fact that the Sun's path through the zodiac changes over time.

That means there are now two sets of dates for your birth sign. The *tropical dates* are the original Babylonian dates; the *sidereal dates* tell you where the Sun actually appears as it moves along its annual path.

For July 27, the tropical sign is **Leo** and the sidereal sign is **Cancer**.

Leo

Tropical July 23 to August 22
Sidereal August 16 to September 15

Leo is one of the earliest recognizable constellations, with its stars forming a sickle or backward question mark. The Mesopotamians, the Persians, the Jews, and the Indians all had a name for the constellation that meant "lion." In Greek mythology, the Nemean lion was impervious to any weapons, but the hero Hercules nevertheless defeated it.

In astrology, Leo is a fire sign, suggesting that Leos are strong-willed and passionate. Leos are supposed to be compatible with Aquarius, Aries, and Sagittarius, but not with Gemini, Capricorn, or Pisces.

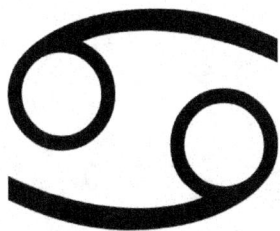

Cancer

Tropical June 21 to July 22
Sidereal July 16 to August 15

The Greek word for "crab" is Καρκινος (Karkinos), later Latinized as carcinus, which evolved into our word cancer. In Greek mythology. In one telling, when Hercules was battling the Hydra, Zeus's wife Hera sent Karkinos to distract the hero, but Hercules kicked it with such force that it was thrown into the sky, becoming a constellation. (Some say that Hercules crushed the crab with his foot and that Hera placed the crab in the night sky as a reward for its service.)

Because of the association with the disease, some astrologers refer to those born under the sign of Cancer as "moon children," because the ruling planet of Cancer is the Moon.

Cancers (or Moon Children) are supposed to be loyal, dependable, caring, and adaptable, but can also be moody, self-pitying, and oversensitive. Cancers are supposed to be particularly compatible with Scorpios, Piceans, and other Cancers.

Illustration by Edward Penfield

What Day of the Week is July 27?

On what day of the week does July 27 fall?

Surprisingly, this isn't an easy question. Because the calendar year is 365 days long (366 in leap years), it doesn't divide evenly by the seven days of the week.

Also, the Earth goes around the Sun in about 365-1/4 days, so a calendar tends to drift over time. That's why the same date falls on different weekdays in different years.

This is made even more complicated by a change in calendars that took place in 1582. Our modern calendar has its roots in ancient Rome, in a calendar reform conducted by Julius Caesar. Caesar commissioned mathematicians to attack the problem, and they came up with the idea of leap years, and thus standardized the calendar for centuries to come. This was called the Julian calendar.

Over time, however, the small errors in Caesar's calculation compounded. That's why Pope Gregory XIII commissioned the Gregorian calendar, used in most of the world today. Some countries converted in 1582, when the calendar was first developed; some converted later; other still haven't changed.

Gregorian and Julian aren't the only types of calendars. The Hebrew year, the Islamic year, and many other calendars are used in different parts of the world and among different people.

You can convert Gregorian dates to other calendars, including the Hebrew calendar, the Islamic calendar, and even the Mayan calendar by visiting the Fourmilab Calendar Converter at http://www.fourmilab.ch/documents/calendar/.

Chinese calendar systems are quite complex and have changed several times; a full discussion is far beyond the scope of this book. If you're interested, you can find information here: http://www.hermetic.ch/cal_stud/chinese_cal.htm.

On Names and Dates

Historians use "CE" (Common Era) and "BCE" (Before the Common Era) instead of the more common "AD" (Anno Domini, or Year of Our Lord) and "BC" (Before Christ), reflecting the fact that the year-numbering system established by the Gregorian calendar is used throughout the world in many countries not culturally Christian.

The CE/BCE designation dates back to at least 1708, and has been adopted as a standard by the United Nations and the Universal Postal Union. Because this series of books covers events and people of all nations and cultures, we use the CE/BCE terms.

The abbreviation "O.S." ("Old Style") and "N.S." ("New Style") on some dates refers to the fact that the Russian Empire (in particular) did not switch from the Julian to the Gregorian calendar at the same time as the rest of Europe, and therefore some figures and events have two dates.

Also, in the Julian calendar in England in the 16th century, the year began on March 25 rather than January 1. To avoid confusion with Gregorian dates, dates between January and March were often written using both years.

People and events whose original names are not in the Western alphabet have their native names (where possible) in the appropriate script shown in parenthesis. If you are using an e-reader to access an electronic version of this book, all characters don't always display on all devices.

A 50-year brass perpetual calendar.

Quote of the Day

"Time is an illusion, lunchtime doubly so."

Douglas Adams,
from *The Hitchhiker's Guide to the Galaxy*

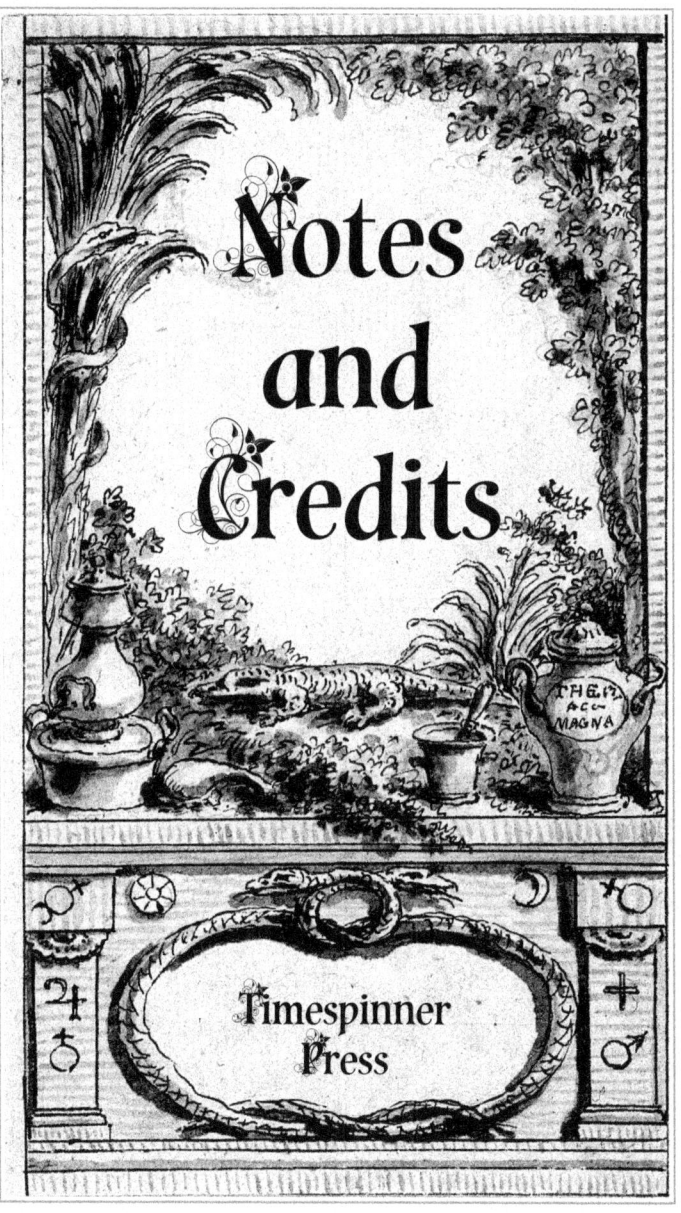

Notes
and
Credits

Timespinner
Press

Cartoon by John T. McCutcheon

Copyright, Credit, and Contact

Follow Us

Our blog "This Day in History" (http://
timespinnerpress.com/this-day-in-history/) features short
articles on events and people associated with each day, and
updates several times each week. Also subscribe to the
"Quote of the Day" at http://timespinnerpress.com/quote-
of-the-day/. You can get daily links by following us on
Facebook at TimespinnerPress, or on Twitter as
@sidewisethinker.

Contact Us

Find an error or a format problem? Want information about
the series, about us, or about when the volume for your
special day might be available? Please email us at
editor@timespinnerpress.com. (We also take requests if your
special day isn't yet complete. Please give us at least six
weeks' notice if possible.)

Sources

We owe a great debt to Wikipedia, which is our first stop for
research. We attempt to make independent confirmation of
all important dates and facts through a variety of other
sources.

Other sources we frequently use include the Library of
Congress; "on this day" listings from *Encyclopedia Britannica*,
the *New York Times*, and the BBC; Omniglot for the names of
months in other languages; *Chase's Calendar of Events*; and, of
course, the always essential Google.

All art and photographs are either in the public domain, used under a Creative Commons license, or with a "fair use" justification, and most frequently come from Wikimedia Commons and the Library of Congress Prints and Photographs Division.

Attribution is provided where possible, or as requested by the copyright owner, or when there is particular historical significance, listed below. For information about any particular illustration or photograph, please contact us.

Credits

1. The 1786 painting of Sarah Siddons and John Phillip Kemble in *Macbeth* is by Thomas Beach, and is located in the Garrick Club, London. It is in the public domain because its copyright has expired.

2. The illustration of the month of July used on the back cover is from the French Gothic illuminated manuscript *Les Très Riches Heures du duc de Berry* by the Limbourg Brothers, Jean Colombe, and an intermediate painter whose name is lost to history. It is in the public domain because its copyright has expired.

3. The box graphic used on the first page is from a 1916 pamphlet entitled "Divorce versus Democracy" authored by G. K. Chesterton, originally published in London by the Society of St. Peter and St. Paul. It is in the public domain in the US because it was published prior to 1923, and is in the public domain in all countries (including the country of origin) in which the copyright time is the author's life plus 70 years or less.

4. The graphic design for the section pages in this book is from a design originally created for a pharmacy label. It is courtesy of Wellcome Images (ICV No 11073, photo V0010813), and is used here under CC BY-SA 4.0.

5. The illustration of Macbeth besieging a castle is from *Scotland's Story* by H. E. Marshall, first published in 1907. It is in the public domain because its copyright has expired.

6. The illustration of Macbeth of Scotland by John Hall is in the public domain because it is more than 70 years old.

7. The 1557 woodcut from *Holinshed's Chronicles* is is the public domain because its copyright has expired.

8. The 1800 painting of William Shakespeare by William Blake can be found in the Manchester City Gallery. It is in the public domain because its copyright has expired.

9. The photograph of General Mark Clark signing the Korean armistice agreement is in the public domain as a work taken by an employee or soldier of the US government as part of that person's official duties. It is courtesy US Navy Museum.

10. The photographer and original source of the 1953 photograph of Kim Il-sung signing the Korean armistice agreement is unknown. The work is in the public domain in Korea, its country of origin, under Articles 39 to 44 of the Copyright Act of the Republic of Korea because its copyright has expired.

11. The circa 1796 painting *La Nuit du 9 au 10 thermidor an II, Arrestation de Robespierre* by Jean-Joseph-François Tassaert can be found in the Carnavalet Museum, Paris. It is in the public domain because its copyright has expired.

12. The December 1944 photograph of American POWs is in the public domain as a work taken by an employee or soldier of the US government as part of that person's official duties. It is courtesy Defense Imagery, VIRIN HD-SN-99-02730.

13. The cropped screenshot from the 1952 film *Road to Bali* is is in the public domain because it was published in the United States between 1923 and 1963 and although there may or may not have been a copyright notice, the copyright was not renewed.

14. The 1860 painting *L'Assassinat de Marat/Charlotte Corday* by Paul-Jacques-Aimé Baudry is courtesy Musée des Beaux-Arts de Nantes (accession number 802). It is in the public domain because its copyright has expired.

15. The 1975 publicity photograph of the *All in the Family* cast is in the public domain because it was first published in the United States between 1923 and 1977 without a copyright notice. Typically, publicity photographs are not copyrighted because of the way in which they are intended to be used.

16. The 2013 photograph of Alex Rodriguez was taken by Glenn Brunette, and is used here under CC BY-SA 2.0.

17. The photograph of stamps showing skater Peggy Fleming is in the public domain, because stamps in Paraguay are in the public domain.

18. The 1962 publicity photograph from the television show *Mister Ed* is in the public domain because it was first published in the United States between 1923 and 1977 without a copyright notice. Typically, publicity photographs are not copyrighted because of the way in which they are intended to be used.

19. The 1939 official engagement photograph of Mohammad Reza Pahlavi is in the public domain in Iran, its country of origin, because its copyright has expired according to the 1970 Law for the Protection of Authors, Composers, and Artists Rights.

20. The photograph of General Claire Chennault with pilots of the 23rd Fighter Group was taken sometime between 1943 and 1945. It is in the public domain as a work taken by an employee or soldier of the US government as part of that person's official duties.

21. The photograph of Gertrude Stein by Carl Van Vechten is part of a collection donated to the Library of Congress (digital ID van.5a52650), and according to the Library, there are no known copyright restrictions on the use of this work.

22. The cropped trailer screenshot from the film *North by Northwest* is in the public domain because it was first published in the United States between 1923 and 1977 without a copyright notice.

23. The American Tobacco Company baseball card of Joe Tinker was published sometime between 1909 and 1911, and is in the public domain because its copyright has expired. It is courtesy of the Benjamin K. Edwards Collection, Library of Congress.

24. The 1912 American Tobacco Company baseball card of Smoky Joe Wood is in the public domain because its copyright has expired.

25. The 1933 Goudey baseball card of Travis Jackson is in the public domain because it was published in the United States between 1923 and 1963 and although there may or may not

have been a copyright notice, the copyright was not renewed.

26. The 1933 Goudey baseball card of Rick Ferrell is in the public domain because it was published in the United States between 1923 and 1963 and although there may or may not have been a copyright notice, the copyright was not renewed.

27. The 2013 photograph of a wreath laying at the Korean War Veterans Memorial was taken by SPC Lance Philpot. Its is in the public domain as a work taken by an employee or soldier of the US government as part of that person's official duties. It is courtesy Defense Imagery, VIRIN 130727-A-LL711-003.

28. The photograph of a Ford Model A ice cream van was taken at the Henry Ford Museum by Alf van Beem, who released the image into the public domain.

29. The painting *Los Zancos* by Francisco Goya was painted between 1791 and 1792, and is in the public domain because its copyright has expired. The original can be found in the Prado Museum, Madrid.

30. The painting "July" is from the *Brevarium Grimani*, circa 1510, and is in the public domain because its copyright has expired.

31. The photograph of a ruby was released into the public domain by its creator.

32. The photograph of a water lily at Kew Gardens was taken by "Dinkum," who released it into the public domain under the CC0 1.0 dedication.

33. The 1821 painting "Study of an Elm Tree" by John Constable is in the public domain because its copyright has expired. The painting is in the collection of the Victoria & Albert Museum, London.

34. The celestial sphere is from *Scenography of the Ptolemaic Cosmography*, by Johannes van Loon, based on Andreas Cellarius's *Harmonia Macrocosmica*, 1660. It is in the public domain because its copyright has expired.

35. The 1906 automobile calendar is by Edward Penfield, and is in the collection of the Library of Congress Prints and Photographs Division. It is in the public domain because its copyright has expired.

36. The 50-year perpetual calendar photograph is in the public domain.

37. The cartoon by John T. McCutcheon is from his 1905 collection *The Mysterious Stranger and Other Cartoons* by John T. McCutcheon. It is in the public domain because its copyright has expired.

License Description and Terms

Aside from material purely in the public domain, photographs and other material in this book are used under specific licenses permitting free use, usually with an attribution requirement. For full text and terms of these licenses, click or enter the appropriate links below. If you believe there is an error in the copyright status or attribution of any of these images, please email us.

- Creative Commons Attribution 2.0 Generic (CC-BY 2.0): http://creativecommons.org/licenses/by/2.0/deed.en
- Creative Commons Attribution-Share Alike 3.0 Generic (CC-BY-SA 3.0): http://creativecommons.org/licenses/by-sa/3.0/
- Creative Commons Attribution-Share Alike 2.5 Generic (CC-BY-SA 2.5): http://creativecommons.org/licenses/by-sa/2.5/deed.en
- Creative Commons Attribution-Share Alike 2.0 Generic (CC-BY-SA 2.0): http://creativecommons.org/licenses/by/2.0/deed.en
- Creative Commons Attribution-Share Alike 1.0 Generic (CC-BY-SA 1.0): http://creativecommons.org/licenses/by-sa/1.0/deed.en
- CC0 1.0 Universal (CC0 1.0) Public Domain Dedication (CC0 1.0) http://creativecommons.org/publicdomain/zero/1.0/deed.en
- GNU Free Documentation License (GFDL): http://en.wikipedia.org/wiki/Wikipedia:Text_of_the_GNU_Free_Documentation_License
- License Art Libre (Free Art License): http://artlibre.org

Other Books from Timespinner Press

The Story of a Special Day
Michael Dobson

A series of (eventually) 366 volumes covering everything that happened on your special day! Events, births, deaths, quotes, holidays, and much more. It's like a birthday card they'll never throw away!

US$7.95 print / US$2.99 ebook.

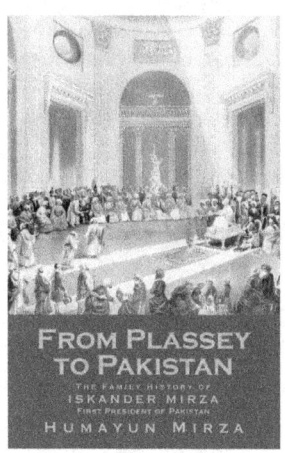

From Plassey to Pakistan
Humayun Mirza

The history of British Colonial India and the formation of Pakistan from the unique perspective of the son of Pakistan's first president and last of the royal line of Bengal, Bihar, and Orissa! This unique historical document tells the inside story of this distinguished family, including the detailed story of the coup that toppled his father from power!

US$27.95 print

A Whole New Navy: America's War in the Pacific

Miles Durr

The most comprehensive and detailed description of America's naval war in the Pacific ever—every battle, every ship, every task force and every task group from Pearl Harbor through the Japanese surrender! A must-have for the collection of every World War II buff!

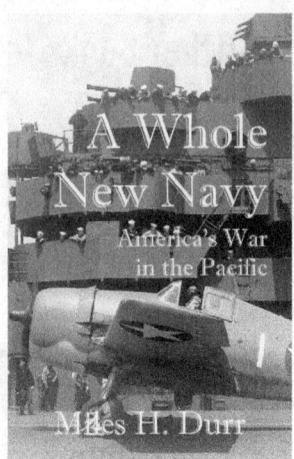

US$29.95 print

Improbable History: The Weird, the Obscure, and the Strangely Important

edited by Michael Dobson

From the birth of Western civilization to the rescue of Apollo 13, from the Leaning Tower of Pisa to Florence's Duomo, history has often turned on small, improbable details. Whatever happened to the ancient Samaritan people? Why did a fortuitous rainstorm allow the British to conquer India? How did an air raid in Italy lead to the development of chemotherapy? What happened when Albert Einstein met Adolf Hitler on the streets of Berlin? How did the Japanese manage to attack the US mainland using balloons? A cast of award-winning writers tackle some of the strangest tales in history!

US$19.95 print

www.ingramcontent.com/pod-product-compliance
Lightning Source LLC
Chambersburg PA
CBHW060208290526
45789CB00003B/1209